It's as SIMPLE as
WHERE YOU LIVE

Barbara,

Such a wonderful

Spirit you are!!

Thanks for believing

in what we do!

It's as SIMPLE as WHERE YOU LIVE

A Guide for Beginning the Journey into Eldercare

Carol J. Chiarito

Paperback: ISBN: 978-1-939758-80-4
eBook: ISBN 978-1-939758-81-1

For information contact:
www.CarematchAmerica.com
Carol@CarematchAmerica.com

Library of Congress Control Number: 2014905065

To my mom, Doris Jean Leighton

You took me into your life as an infant and adopted me as your own. You have shown me how to be a strong woman, to work hard for what I want, and how to laugh at myself along the way. Thanks, Mom, for being my inspiration for my book and Carematch America, and more importantly, for allowing us to spend this precious time together during your golden years.

CONTENTS

An Invitation

My mom passed away on April 1st, 2013. She'd had a stroke a few days before, followed by a heart attack. She screamed her last words, as she had lost her speech by then.

"I love you!" she screamed to my dad, after sixty-three years of marriage. He had devoted himself to taking care of her, and had abandoned all other activities to do so. He was with her until the very end. And then she told him she loved him and passed on.

Reality settled in. My dad had to move out of the apartment he had lived in for the past twenty-nine years. My brother, sister, and I had to help him as he was both devastated and lost. All of us were mired in questions that seemed impossible to answer at the time. Where should he live? What did he want to do? What did he like? In the wake of my mother's death, we were all moving through life as if in a thick fog.

We spent months looking at different centers and communities, traveling around from place to place. The marketing people at each place wanted *their* facility to be the one that suited my dad. But for the most part, they ignored his wishes and our concerns, tirelessly hawking what they had to offer instead. There was no sense of consumer-based care: just an insatiable hunger to *sell sell sell*.

The search took ten months. After exhaustive research and countless visits, we finally found his dream place. We were all worn out by then, tired and disheartened, but so very grateful we finally found a place Dad could call home.

I wish now that we had known about Carol's work. Carematch America would have saved us so many months that could have been dedicated to spending quality time with my father, celebrating and cherishing the last years of his life. At eighty-four he is now happy, but we will never recapture the time spent trying to find him a place of his own.

It's As Simple As Where You Live is a gift for any family, a guide to caring for the elders in our lives with wisdom, heart, and compassion. Read this book, and enjoy the time you have with your loved one. You'll be glad you did.

–Pierre G Boissé
Montreal, Canada

Acknowledgments

Karin Kyte for the cover photo.

Jim Morgan, Harriet Warren, and Steve Thomas for sharing their stories with me and allowing me to share with the world.

Christopher Hall, my son who has helped me create Carematch America, and will one day pick my nursing home.

My husband, Rick, and my son, Vinny, who listen to my stories over and over and allow me to travel and meet the great people in the world and move my company forward.

Special thanks to the Pioneer Network (www.pioneernetwork.org) and The Eden Alternative (www.edenalt.org).

Keep It Consumer-Centered:
Changing the Way People Find Care

*F*OR SOME FAMILIES, it happens gradually. For others, the change comes almost overnight. But no matter the timeframe, when we finally understand that our parents are aging, it can come as a shock. One day the people who once cared for us—raised us, fed and clothed us, provided for us, and mentored us—suddenly turn to us and say, "I need your help."

It's not always a question of a drastic change in independence. It's true that sudden illness can mean our elders live alone safely one day and require full-time, nursing-level care the next. But often the change is more gradual, and deciding how to sift through the options is far from easy. The world of senior housing is vast, from retirement communities—where residents still drive, cook for themselves, play tennis, and swim—to different levels of independent living facilities, assisted living facilities, and nursing homes. When it comes time for you and your parent to consider the options, the task can be daunting.

Accepting and navigating this life change is challenging for all involved, on a physical and emotional level certainly, but often on a logistical and financial one as well. And all too often, there are few, if any, signposts to guide us on our way. Not only are we starting down a path that is new to us, it can often feel like we're in territory that is uncharted altogether—that we're the only ones who've ever traveled it before.

I offer this book to you as a signpost on that challenging path. It is an assurance that, despite the twists and turns of a less-than-perfect system of eldercare, you are not alone. In fact, the opposite is true: we all share a strikingly similar story.

Whether you are caring for both parents, just Mom or Dad, or a beloved grandparent, aunt, uncle, or family friend; whether you have siblings or a spouse, partner, or adult child to share the responsibility, or whether you are the sole caretaker; whether you live in New York City or San Francisco, Toronto or San Antonio; whether your elder is a thousand miles away, down the street, or in your own home, there are elements of this journey that we all share.

When I set out on this path with my mother, we were amazed to find how difficult it was not only to find information but also to understand the information we did find. We were bombarded with jargon that was meaningless to us and flooded with solicitations from communities that didn't fit my mother's needs at all. The trouble was that these facilities were not marketing themselves in a consumer-oriented way. They weren't challenging themselves to consider our perspective.

When I shared my experience with others, I discovered that my mother and I had a common problem. A friend of mine, who also lives here in Colorado, had been searching for a place for her mother in Seattle, Washington, and was running up against the same confusion—compounded by distance and her inability to actually visit different locations and see the options available.

Another friend in Colorado had been working to find home health care providers for his elder parents, who still live on the family farm in Iowa. He'd solved the distance problem—expensively and inconveniently—by flying or driving out to Iowa every month ... but he was no closer to finding the right solution for his parents.

For each of us, and for many others in similar situations, it was impossible to even know where to begin—let alone spend the time away from work and family to research the possibilities.

The average consumer simply doesn't understand this industry or the differences between the overwhelming choices for eldercare. I know this because at the beginning of my own journey, I was sitting exactly where you are: lost and frustrated. I didn't know where to turn for help.

Since then, my mother and I have found a solution that works for her, and out of the knowledge I gained in that process, I've created a company to educate the public on the options available to them. In *It's as Simple as Where You Live*, I want to share my personal experience with you. My hope is that my experience will help give children and other caregivers a sense of direction and convey a message of hope. Think of this book as a starting point for discovering where your own path lies, what your options are, and some tips on getting through it.

I am a consumer who has walked in your shoes: I worked hard to find good care for my beloved parent. I've experienced the day-to-day issues my mother goes through, and I have learned there are many choices out there—and not always the ones that are readily apparent. Times have changed since our grandparents and great-grandparents were in "nursing homes." There are ways of starting the search process early, communicating with those around you, and knowing what you are looking for that will ease the burden, making this time of life less stressful for everyone.

Knowing what you want before the time comes is key, so is understanding the system and the choices it offers. I'm here to act as a guide along the journey—to shine a light on your path. I hope it's both a help and a comfort.

All my best,
Carol Chiarito
Founder and President

CHAPTER 1

Mom and Me: Our Journey through My Mother's Steps of Care

*M*Y MOM IS the ultimate planner. In that sense, I was extremely lucky as the adult child of an elder parent. My mom had the impulse to plan ahead, to go through options and carefully select the one that was most appealing, that suited her best, like that perfect dress or pair of shoes. And that meant she was the one who first started a tough conversation.

"You know," she said to me one day, "I would like to start shopping for assisted living. One of these days I'm going to need it, so I'd like to get an idea of what's out there, what they look like, and how they work. That way I can have one picked out for myself, and you won't have to decide for me."

If Mom hadn't brought it up, I'm not sure I would have. Even in adulthood, we tend to follow our parents' lead. As they begin to age, and life calls upon us more and more to turn the tables of the caretaking relationship, it can be uncomfortable, awkward, and even painful. It's understandable, then, that we have difficulty being proactive in terms of our parents' care—we tend to wait for the opportunity to present itself, rather than create the opportunity ahead of time.

So I was lucky Mom thought of assisted living first. And I was happy to be her shopping partner. Unfortunately, neither of us had any idea just what we were getting ourselves into.

We live in the small city of Pueblo, Colorado, with a population of about 125,000 people. Perhaps because of the community's size, the senior care facilities in the city aren't particularly motivated to make their presence known. "Everyone knows where we are!" they assume. "We've been here fifty years!"

That's usually not the case. These facilities certainly weren't on my radar before it occurred to me Mom might need one. So, being a bit traditionalist, I started with the good old Yellow Pages.

However, one glance was enough to tell me this wasn't going to be easy. We found page after page of listings for all types of eldercare communities, facilities, and services. There was no way we'd have time to call or visit all of them—and we wanted to be fully informed before making such a big decision.

So, we turned to the next step: searching on the Internet.

Of course, Google and other search engines are only as smart as the keywords you enter, and at that time, we were woefully deficient in keywords. We really only had two questions: Will the facility allow her to bring her dog? And will they let her smoke?

Those were our only criteria! We had no idea just how complex our options were, so we couldn't even begin to get specific about what we were asking for.

The Internet turned out not to be all that different from the Yellow Pages: We ended up with a list of names, with no real insight into the places behind those names. Almost as if they were following some unwritten code, each website showed us a photo of the facility's front door. But what happens *behind* that door?

Eventually, I came across a website that required me to enter my personal information, including my name and contact phone number, before I could even begin searching the listings. Hoping I'd find some worthwhile information, I entered the required data.

My phone started ringing right away, and didn't stop for forty-five minutes.

In less than an hour, more than twenty-five communities had called to place their bids for the "business" of caring for my mother. I was frustrated, to say the least—and by the fifteenth or sixteenth phone call, several community placement and admissions employees had started to share my frustration as I became less than cordial.

Somehow I had thought the process would be like house hunting. I would compile a list of three or four places based on my research, and my mother and I would spend an afternoon visiting. But even the basic step of creating a list of viable options and setting up appointments was out of my reach. I still didn't even know if anyone would allow my mother to bring her dog!

After three months of research, I suddenly learned I hadn't even been searching the right category of facilities. We had assumed my mom should look at assisted living, when in fact this is a level of care that elders have to qualify for. Elders have to be evaluated by a doctor to determine if they need assistance in the activities of *daily living*, which are getting out of bed, getting out of a chair, bathing, using the bathroom, and dressing. If a doctor certifies that a person cannot perform two or more of these five activities unassisted, then he or she qualifies for assisted living.

Three months had come and gone before we understood that assisted living wasn't appropriate for my mom; we should have been looking for independent living options. Independent living is for people who don't need assistance with daily activities—they're perfectly independent; they just want to live in a more social setting. At that point, we'd never even heard of independent living! We were flying without a net.

Almost serendipitously, our discovery of the difference between assisted and independent living coincided with our discovery of a brand new independent living facility being built about a mile from where my mom was living. There was a sign out front, "*Sign up today!*" And that's what we did.

On our first tour of the building, my mom liked it so much she signed a contract right then and there. She had been living in a little patio home in a retirement cul-de-sac. Even though she didn't need any help, living in a house by herself got lonely for her. She was thrilled by the idea of having a community, all in one building—and having meals prepared for her.

The transition was not easy. It took my mom at least a year to feel settled and comfortable socially—and during that time, it wasn't just the new living arrangement she was adjusting to. She was also dealing with the expected (and some unexpected) shifts and changes of growing older.

She had decided to pay one hundred dollars a year so that she could park her little Toyota in the facility's garage and have it at the ready if she wanted to go out on her own. But her eyesight was changing, and realistically, she wasn't comfortable driving anymore. She liked the idea of having her car there and having the option if she wanted it, but she never actually wanted it.

Every now and then she'd tell me, "I'm on my way to drive to Walgreens by myself."

And I would say, "Go ahead, Mom, if you think you're safe."

And she never would.

As much as she was beginning to enjoy the company,

she was going through a process of adjusting to a new life stage. And I was adjusting along with her.

My husband and I live out in the country, and we loved to have my mom over. My family comes from a ranch, and we could see how much my mom liked to sit on our back patio, which faces a hay field on one side and a pasture with my neighbor's three or four horses on the other. My mom loved to watch the horses, just looking out into the wild blue yonder.

I started to wonder if having my mom in my home would be better for her and better for our family than having her in the independent living facility in town. So after a while, I convinced her to move in with me. My husband and I moved into the guest bedroom, and we turned our master bedroom into a little apartment for Mom.

I was excited! I could have my mom with me, where I could monitor her eating and her health. And at first, she was excited to "help" me. That's the thing about moms: They've been taking care of you your whole life. All of a sudden, not only was she no longer taking care of me, she was starting to worry she wouldn't be able to take care of *herself* anymore.

When she moved in, she wanted so much to help me. She wanted to do all the dishes and do my laundry. And I was telling her, "Mom, you don't need to do that. Let *me* help *you*." In retrospect, I wish I had given her more things to do around the house; I realize now she was trying to hold on to that part of herself and feel that she was needed.

Two weeks after moving her whole life and all her possessions out to my house, she said, "Ugh, I'm not happy here. It's boring. I'm going to move back!"

"What?" I asked.

"I miss playing Bingo and getting my hair done. I miss having lunch with my girlfriends," she said.

We had talked about this before she moved out. She understood that my husband and I would be at work all day. So, I told her, "Let's give it *at least* two more months."

I thought two months would give her the time to settle down and become accustomed to the change. No chance. Instead, she was counting down the days like a kid counts down to Christmas!

"When did you say I was moving?" she asked me— every single day. "Should we start packing?"

Finally I had to acquiesce. We packed everything up all over again, and moved her back to the independent living facility. As we were moving her back in, I could hear the women on her hall telling each other, "Doris Jean's back! Doris Jean's back! Did you hear Doris Jean's back?"

That's when it clicked for me. This process had nothing to do with what was best for me; it was about her. I had thought what would be best for my mom was for her to move into my world. But I realized, in that moment, that my world is not Mom's world. She didn't want to watch my TV shows and eat my food and have only me and my family for company. She wanted to make her own choices and have her own life.

I had to learn that the important thing was not what I wanted for my mom, it was what she wanted for herself. That was what she deserved to have for this portion of a long, loving, successful life. To be the happiest she could be.

Many months after this moving back and forth with my mother, I met a woman from Texas who fervently wanted to invest in my business of helping match elders with living situations. The reason she felt so committed to the idea was that her father had committed suicide because he was so lonely in his home. They had thought that the best thing for him would be to let him keep his home, but his friends were gone and his daughter lived in a town far enough away that she couldn't drop in for coffee. In the end, he just didn't want to do it anymore.

What I hadn't recognized—and what my investor hadn't had the information to see until it was too late—was that the social aspect of our elders' living arrangements is just as crucial as the cooking, cleaning, medical care, and other logistics that we pay so much attention to.

In my mother's independent living facility—where she still is today—the residents have a ball. It's like a dorm for seniors! They have a pub and a happy hour every Friday at three o'clock. There is a movie theater with films two or three times a week. The building has an on-site hairdresser and workout room. Everything my mom needs to conduct a social, engaged life is right there at her fingertips.

Many of us have terrible memories of our grandparents' nursing homes. When we talk about senior living, there is a connotation of putting our loved ones in a "home." We imagine smelly, drab places where people miss their families and their former lives, and where they feel pushed away and forgotten.

What my journey with my mom taught me was that we have so many more options today. Yes, it is possible to have twenty-four/seven skilled nursing care—the kind of service you imagine when you hear the words "nursing home." But this is not the only level of care available. Depending on your family's needs and how your parent or elder envisions life, you can have anything from in-home assistance providing the occasional meal or grocery shopping to a full-care, live-in facility.

Today we have options. There are tailored services that fit with what your parent or elder is able to provide for themselves and what they need or want to have provided for them. And beyond that, services exist to help our elders continue to feel connected to their social circles, to feel like they matter and have a role in their family's lives and in the world.

Navigating these signals can be difficult, and it's easy to get tripped up. What care do our parents truly need? How should we respond to those signals? In the following chapters, we'll discuss some ways to walk this journey. But first, let's make sure you, your parents, and everyone else in your family is on the same page.

CHAPTER *2*

The Kitchen-Table Talk: Getting Your Mom, Dad, and Siblings on the Same Page

STEVE: MY PARENTS were still living on the family farm in Iowa. My dad was eighty-five and my mom was a few years younger. That's when we started having some issues—we were seeing some red flags that my parents weren't taking such good care of themselves.

The doctor suggested we sit down with our counselor. "We" included my parents, my sister, my brother, and me, as well as our spouses. Because I'm in Colorado and my brother's in a different part of Iowa, we all got on a conference call. We talked about the issues my parents faced living on a farm, everything from the rugs on the floors to the steps they had to go up and down every day. That first call was basically an orientation: the counselor wanted us to be more aware of the potential issues my parents faced. We weren't thinking about this stuff yet, because we're not that age and have't had to think about it. But after that initial call we had a much better idea.

The counselor told us that if anything happened to either one of our parents, both of them would end up in a nursing home. Neither one of them could handle the farm by themselves. Together they could fake it, but as soon as there was one bad fall or one serious accident, they'd both be forced to look at other options.

There were some big safety issues, like the fact that both my parents were still driving. I'll tell you something: if you want to have some fun, sit down with your parents and have a counselor ask them what they think of their driving. Then ask each of their kids what *they* think of their parents' driving. The answers are likely to be very different, and at that point there's nowhere to hide.

So my mother was given a letter from the doctor saying, "Thou shalt not drive at night, or more than ten miles in any direction." But it took my wife and my niece, who's an RN, to finally zero in on the fact that my father's medication had not been matched up properly by his doctor, and it was not being taken properly by my father. And my mom was aiding and abetting him—so you get a sense of the whole picture.

These were the sorts of issues we were dealing with. After that first "kitchen-table talk," we brought in some nonprofessional care to help with cleaning and cooking, but both my parents successfuly chased her off. They didn't think they needed it and my dad didn't want to spend the money. Then we brought in an RN to supervise the medication. That went all right for about three days, at which time the nurse left the bill on the kitchen counter, so my parents knew exactly how much they'd been charged and exactly how little she'd actually been there. That individual was not invited back, either.

That was the straw that broke the camel's back. My mother was forgetting how to cook; she was burning pans and she wasn't cleaning the house as well as she used to. The medication mismanagement had become a major issue, to the point where my parents were having to schedule doctors' appointments because they couldn't figure out why they were having problems. One thing led to another, and my brother, sister, and I simply weren't capable of keeping track of all of it. My sister lived on a farm a few miles away, but even then, we just couldn't monitor everything.

Luckily, my siblings and I were all on the same page. I spent a good few days on Google, trying to find out what services were available to us in a small farming community in Iowa. My sister was our "on-site" person: since she lived closest to Mom and Dad, she was able to visit the communities we had researched. After that, my brother and I spent another day putting together an analysis of the diffferent communities, what they could provide, and how much they cost.

We ended up with a completely different answer than what we thought we would end up with. At first glance, the nicest of the communities we looked at—incidentally, the one my mother liked the most—appeared to be the most expensive, but it was actually the best value because of the way they put their package together. We would not have known that had my brother and I not put in a good bit of work.

I only understand this now, in hindsight: having those talks early on put my sister and brother and I on the same wavelength. We understood the issues we were solving for and what my parents really needed, and we're fortunate in that we pretty much agreed on everything. The upside was that those conversations got us all back in touch, those conversations, creating an ongoing family discussion about my parents' aging.

Maybe your family is like Steve's: you're in regular communication with your siblings and are already on the same page about your parents' care. Or maybe you're out of touch, not really involved in the fabric of each other's lives. Maybe you don't even *like* your siblings all that much, and the last thing you want to do is invite them all over for a family powwow.

The thing that came up again and again in my interviews was that this process is rarely smooth for any family. It is emotional enough to watch your parent's life change, but beyond that, every family has its own particular dynamics and its own "baggage," if you will. Discovering that our parents are no longer as independent as they once were has a way of unzipping that baggage and shaking it loose all over the house.

That's what happened to my family. My experience

of pulling my brothers together to discuss my mom's care has not been a bed of roses. You might recognize aspects of your own family dynamics in mine—and you might benefit from the solutions we managed to come to together. Because no matter how you'd describe your unique family situation, the kitchen-table talk is a vital part of the process of helping your parents transition into their elder years.

The roots of my mother's changing health go all the way back to 1987, when she and my father were in a car accident. Sadly, he passed away, and she survived—with a damaged hip. She had to have that hip replaced about ten years later, and about ten years after that she had to have her other hip replaced. Fast forward another ten years or so, and it was time for her first hip replacement to be "updated." The metal parts added to a hip to reconstruct it don't last forever, and it was time to "replace the replacement," so to speak.

My mother had once been a very strong and healthy woman at about 150 pounds, but by the time she went in for that third hip surgery, she was 108 pounds dripping wet. She was simply getting older, and two major surgeries had already taken their toll. She'd become a tiny little woman, and her bones were very brittle.

In most hip replacements, a metal rod is inserted into the top of the thigh bone. Her original rod (shaft) had broken through her leg bone and was protruding. When the doctors began to remove that rod so that they could replace it, the thigh bone around it simply started to disintegrate. It was too brittle to withstand the procedure. The doctors had to patch cadaver bone into her femur to hold the new metal rod in place. The entire surgery took seven or eight hours, and my mom never really bounced back from it. It was an ordeal, to say the least.

I am the youngest of four—I have three older brothers. Taking care of my mother after her surgery largely fell to me because she and I both lived in Pueblo. My family is from a very small town in Eastern Colorado. About seven years ago, my mom decided to leave her home there and move closer to her children (my three brothers now live in Northern Colorado and Southern Wyoming). So she looked first in their areas and to be fair came to look in Pueblo (Southern Colorado) where

I live. She found a beautiful patio home in Pueblo and bought it on the spot the weekend after Thanksgiving. She was in her new home before Christmas.

Unfortunately, my brothers didn't understand the decision. They saw that our mom was moving away from them and toward me. It caused a rift in our family that hasn't quite healed, even today. My brothers thought I must have coerced her into moving closer to me, but in fact that wasn't true. I was just as surprised as they were, but she told me she liked the smaller city, and she felt more comfortable with me taking care of her. I've since heard many similar stories: in families where there are both sons and daughters, the female child typically becomes the caregiver.

So about a year or so after she moved to Pueblo, the surgery came, and my brothers weren't able to witness the change in our mother as closely as I was. Because Pueblo is a three-hour drive from where they live, they see her only three or four times a year or so. I, on the other hand, was witnessing on a daily basis that my mother's health had dramatically changed.

She couldn't get around as well anymore. She couldn't go outside to her garden and get on her hands and knees to plant and tend to her flowers, which she had always loved. The foods she could tolerate were changing, partly because of the medications she was taking. She would complain to me that nothing tasted good to her anymore. She lost more weight.

It was at that time that she brought up the issue of assisted living with me. Before she had moved to Pueblo, and before the third hip surgery, she was like a different person. She was able to drive anywhere and everywhere on her own—she would take roadtrips to see family without anyone being concerned. She was extremely independent—she was a busybody! This was the Mom my brothers were used to—and they hadn't really come to accept and understand that the new Mom was different.

Unbeknownst to me, my brother in Northern Colorado took my mom to visit some assisted living places near his family. They were trying to coax her to move closer to them. At the same time, I was beginning the search on my own in Southern Colorado, without involving my brothers, which I now consider to be a mistake. At the time I didn't really feel like I needed to include them: Mom had asked me to take the necessary steps, and I was just following her instructions, like a good daughter. Looking back, I see that we were all functioning independently of one another, when we could have joined forces and approached our mom's care as a unified team.

So, when we finally told my brothers that Mom was moving into a community in Pueblo, they hadn't been through the learning and adjusting process that we had. It came out of the blue for them. And they didn't have the benefit of the new knowledge that I had acquired through my research. When they heard that our mother was moving into an independent living community, the message to them sounded more like, "Carol is putting Mom in a 'home.'"

In twenty-twenty hindsight, I understand now that I should have included my brothers in the conversation when our mom first brought it up. I should at least have brought them into the process when we first visited the independent living community she eventually moved into. Instead, I figured I knew what Mom wanted, and that was all that mattered. I didn't factor my brothers' thoughts and feelings into the equation.

As a result, my brothers first saw the independent

living community after Mom had already moved in. They were imagining the horror stories of "grandfather's nursing home"—as I probably would have been before I had the opportunity to educate myself about the levels of care available. So, I'm glad that they encountered a pleasant surprise when they first visited. They were delighted by all the community had to offer, just as Mom and I had been when we first saw the place. They would come and visit and take Mom to the on-site ice cream parlor or have a happy-hour drink at the bar. It was a fairly tame resolution to what could have been a volatile situation.

But that wasn't the end of the matter. My mom is still in the same community today, but that doesn't mean her life has been static in the last three or four years. She and I have both been noticing that her needs are continuing to shift—that moving from independent to assisted living is definitely the next step.

Mom's memory is starting to slip. She sometimes forgets to take her medication—or she sometimes forgets that she has taken it, and overmedicates. Not long ago, she had to be admitted to the hospital because she got confused about which of her pills were which. She and I both learned the hard way that sometimes different batches of the same medication can look totally different. She had a medication for her heart that was produced in flat, brown, oblong pills. When she received the refill, the pills were bright blue and kind of fat. It was the same medication—but the pills didn't even remotely resemble each other.

So, Mom thought I had forgotten to put her pills in her pillbox. She took extras without knowing it—for three days. Luckily, the overdose was quite treatable, and she's fine now. But we have both taken it as an early sign that it's time to start planning ahead for assisted living in the same way we planned ahead for independent living.

This time around, I decided to include my brothers in the conversation. I learned from my mistake when they felt that the independent living facility had been "sprung on" them, and I had also gained enough experience in working with other families to see the pain and stress that not being on the same page at the same time can cause.

So I called a family meeting. For you to accurately picture the scene, you have to know that our Mom's care is not the only bone of contention in my family. Before the meeting, I hadn't spoken to one of my brothers in years; he and I have always been at odds for whatever reason. It was actually difficult to get him to come to the family meeting at all.

He and his wife are Broncos season-ticket holders, and the Broncos happened to be playing on the day of our meeting. They called me to say they probably wouldn't make it. There had been a big mix-up in communication and we hadn't explained fully the intent of the meeting to them. They had been visiting my mother that weekend and were at her house. My other two brothers had driven down three hours just for the meeting, so it was important.

When my sister-in-law called to say they weren't going to stay for the meeting, she also said that IF she was at the meeting, it probably wouldn't be good, because she would end up telling me what she thought of me and how she didn't like how I was caring for Mom. (She had been moving through her own experience with her mother who had Alzheimer's). I explained I felt that would be the best thing that could possibly happen; in fact that was one of the reasons for the meeting in the first place. We all needed to get our feelings out, share what was going on with our mother, and get on the same page.

"I know we've been at odds for a long time," I told her. "I also know you're going through a similar situation with your mother. I would really like to have my brother's input. And Mom would like you to be here as well."

That's right: I played the "Mom card." And it worked. I promised they would be out in time to make the game, and they came!

But from the moment they walked through the door, they were angry. They were huffing and puffing and giving every indication they didn't want to be there. My brother immediately went and got a beer—at ten o'clock in the morning! I knew it was to calm his nerves. He was in my house, on my turf, and it was no secret we didn't get along.

I pulled my oldest brother aside and said, "Why don't you lead this meeting?"

"What am I going to say?" he wanted to know.

There was nothing to do but for me to forge forward—after all, I was the one who had most of the information at that point. I'll be honest: It was hard.

I started by saying, "I know we have problems

between us, but we need to get over it for the sake of Mom." My mother, who was sitting next to me, started to cry. Of course, any time my mom starts crying, I start to cry, too. And this time was no different.

But I kept trying to move things forward.

"Guys," I said, "if I get hit by a bus tomorrow, you need to know what's going on in our mom's life."

I took a deep breath ... and continued with the whole story. When I talked about assisted living, my brothers had an image in their heads: "We're going to strap Mom into a chair in front of the window." And I explained to them, that doesn't really happen in the places we were looking at. I had to begin at the beginning, and redraw the picture for them, telling them what assisted living actually is.

And I explained why we were considering it. "Does Mom need assisted living today? No. Will she need it six months from now? Maybe. If she does, we're all going to be involved in the decision. She wants to lead the charge right now, while she's able to make decisions for herself."

It was like there was a collective exhale in the room. "Oh! Oh, okay, we get it!" they all said. They had been terrified by what they imagined to be what I was planning for Mom—and they had a right to be terrified of that image; it was admittedly unpleasant. But it was also baseless. The only way to eradicate their fear was to eradicate their mistaken idea, and the only way to do that was for us to talk to each other openly and honestly.

The next thing I did was to show them a book: *The Critical Illness/Long Term Care Planner,* published by a company called the Long Term Care Planning Network. In founding my own business, I met and began closely collaborating with Karen Henderson, who founded the Long Term Care Planning Network. In the Planner, Karen has assembled questions that allow families to plan ahead for any change in a parent's situation.

When you use the Planner, you sit down with Mom when she is still doing well, and you write down everything. The book helps you organize every detail, some obvious, and some not so readily apparent—but it's all information that could prove vital. For example, what does Mom want, specifically, for her care? What are her daily habits and activities? What kinds of food does she really dislike? Where does she keep her will? her cash? her bills? What medications does she take? In what dosage? At what time of day?

I used the Planner as a tool in my meeting with my brothers. Mom and I had already filled it out together, and we passed it around the table.

"If something happens to me, any one of you or any other caregiver could pick up this book and start exactly where I left off," I told them.

Again, their response was, "Oh! We get it! This is great."

My brothers started asking questions, and pretty soon Mom started telling stories from the past. And by the end of the meeting, we were all laughing. The beginning had been very, very hard . . . but the conclusion, we all agreed, was a really good thing.

Everyone left saying, "I'm glad we did this. I didn't understand what this was about in the beginning, but now I understand."

The importance of that family conversation was actually twofold: Not only did it fill a purpose logistically by getting us all the information we all really needed to have, but it also helped us all to feel some emotional relief. We were no longer operating on assumptions and worst-case-scenario imaginings, which can sow poison between family members. We all felt so much more comfortable because we had reached an agreement that everyone got to participate in together.

The tensions between my brothers and me haven't disappeared completely; we still have our communication challenges. But for my part, I am no longer interested in keeping them in the dark. I will communicate what is going on with Mom, even if it is a one-sided conversation. They're free to do with that information what they will.

~~> ~~> ~~>

In almost every family with more than one adult child, the role of primary caretaker tends to fall to an individual rather than being split equally among all the siblings. Sometimes it just makes more sense in terms of finances, time management, or where different siblings live in relation to the parents—and sometimes there is just someone who naturally comes forward.

Culturally, this primary caretaker is more often a woman. In families where there is more than one sister, the role tends to default to the oldest sister. In my family, the job fell to me not only because I was the only sister but also because of the knowledge and experience I'd gained professionally.

In other families, the "default choice" might not be the ideal one, and so a more involved and communicative decision-making process becomes necessary. For example, I met a man through my business who has two brothers and no sisters. When their mother was no longer able to live as independently as she had before, the family made a decision together to move her closer to the youngest brother, even though the oldest brother already lived fairly close by. The decision came down to family dynamics, the time the youngest brother had to contribute, and the fact that she had friends near him whom she wanted to be closer to. The decision couldn't just be about what the brothers wanted; it had to factor in what would make their mother happiest socially as well as what would ensure she was well taken care of.

Even once the decision has been made, that doesn't mean the conversation is over. In my family, it is a constant process of re-evaluating, and sometimes I find that emotions continue to come up around the decisions we've already made. I do get frustrated with and angry at my brothers because they aren't here to help me. They live three hours away, so the day-to-day things simply have to fall to me.

And when they do come visit, they get to have just the fun side of being with Mom rather than the less exciting daily details. They can just have a pleasure visit.

I've asked my mom, "How about we let them take you to the grocery store?"

And she looks at me like I've lost my mind. "Why would my sons take me to the grocery store?" she asks. "They don't grocery shop!"

So, I certainly find myself getting angry sometimes that my brothers aren't more engaged. But on the flip side, I also find myself getting defensive when they do try to engage. "Wait a minute, that's my turf!" I think to myself. I want help . . . but I don't want help. It can be very complicated. Because I've been the primary care-taker for so many years, I sometimes think I'm the only one who can do it.

I know my mom so well. When we go out to dinner, she hands me the menu and asks me, "What do I like again?" I remember the things she enjoyed in past dinners. When my brothers used to visit, they would often take her to places where she didn't know what she liked and couldn't eat anything on the menu. They meant well—they just hadn't had the benefit of experience. My brothers have gotten much better about this recently: now when they visit, they take her to places where she can navigate the menu, and they've made an effort to learn what she likes.

Even if one sibling in a family becomes the primary caretaker, however, everyone in the family can and should have a role. It might be something very simple and specific that they do every year even from afar— like making sure insurance is up to date. Or it might be something more regular that requires their presence, their time, their money, or their car—like taking Mom or Dad on a weekly trip to the grocery store or driving to medical appointments.

Deciding what role different family members will play is as much a part of that difficult "kitchen-table talk" as getting clear and honest about your parent's wishes. So, my brothers and I asked each other: Where do you think you fit in best? What help are you able to offer? It's not about helping me, but about helping our Mom. That was the perspective that made the difference for us, and made us all want to be in the game.

Ultimately, that's what caring for an aging family member is: a team sport. Nobody gets to sit on the bench and watch the game. Everyone is going to be involved. But the players do get to decide what positions they play, together, so that the whole court is covered.

❧ ❧ ❧

Not too long ago, my mother and I were driving together. Every now and then, she gets worried that she is taking too much of my time and having to call on me to help her too much. She started to go down that road.

When she gets sad and implies that she's a burden, my response is to try to make her laugh. That's what I did this time around.

I happen to be adopted. My parents had many, many foster children throughout the years, and they adopted me—after having their three biological sons. So, I said to my mom, "I think the reason that God brought me to you was so that we could be here right now. You took care of me at the beginning, when I didn't have anyone to take care of me. And now I'm taking care of you."

Mom paused and thought it over. Then she said, "You know, that could be the reason!"

And together, we laughed.

CHAPTER 3

Give Your Parents What They Want:
Aging on *Their* Terms

*J*IM: WHAT WAS most important to my mother was finding a place where she could participate in group activities—she actually didn't need a lot of care. But so much of what we were finding was geared toward nursing care. It just didn't apply; she didn't need it. That was our biggest struggle: finding a place that would offer a group setting and maybe some food service. That was really all we wanted, and there just wasn't much of it.

In the beginning, my siblings and I felt we were pretty capable of doing a lot of searching on our own. We were trying to do Internet research because we were all located in different places, so it wasn't easy to do site visits. Most of the actual site visits fell to my brother who was in the area. For the rest of us, searching around online, we found that pretty soon all the websites looked the same. We really couldn't get a sense of any individual personality of the places.

Each website had a similar look: "Here's a picture of the dining room; here's a picture of the front door; here's a picture of a typical resident room. We've got very loving staff!" They were all very welcoming once you were in contact with them; it was just a matter of sifting through to find the right place.

We wanted to make sure we weren't overlooking anything, or not considering things that we should consider. So, ultimately we got connected with a service, a nationally affiliated site helping with placements. My one brother who started the process with them lives in Philadelphia, and they gave him an agent in the Philadelphia area. But we were looking for residences in Ohio!

It became very clear to us that the person we were working with didn't know the Ohio area. They were finding things online and referring us. Well, we found those same places online ourselves! We asked to be hooked up with somebody in the Ohio area—and there was resistance to that. I'm assuming the agent was making money off us, and they didn't want to give that up. That struck me as very selfish and not very customer-oriented, especially as someone who has worked in sales. We were already aware from having looked on the Internet ourselves, and the places the agent was recommending weren't in any way meeting our criteria. And yet we're still, more than a year later, getting emails and phone calls, and trying to get off their lists.

It was frustrating. I wish the eldercare industry would take a cue from the real estate industry. I know a lot of realtors. If you look at how they are able to market a home over the Internet, and the visuals and videos they provide, they really give you a good sense of the property. That could probably be incorporated into the search for eldercare, to give people a better sense of what they're looking at.

That first room you walk into where people are sitting around, you know right then the energy of the facility. Not that you decide everything from that first impression ... but boy, that's one heck of a big first impression.

♧ ♧ ♧

The major theme of my journey with my mom has been that we needed to become educated. We had to learn, first of all, that there *are* different levels of care available—that there are so many options these days, above and beyond "your grandfather's nursing home" of yes-teryear. And then from there, we had to start getting specific about what each level of care entailed so that we could make decisions about what Mom needed—both in the present and what she might need in the future.

An organization that I found extremely valuable—and that my company eventually became a value-added Partner with—was The Eden Alternative. They are a descendent of the Pioneer Network, whose vision is for eldercare to move away from provider-driven models of care to more consumer-driven models of care, so that, as their website says, "when our grandparents, parents—and ultimately ourselves—go to a nursing home or other community-based setting it is to thrive, not to decline." I encourage you to check out their excellent homepage at https://www.edenalt.org/ for more information.

Pioneer Network has various other divisions and organizations that subscribe to their philosophy, and ultimately they are all interested in creating a change in the culture of eldercare. Almost every state has a "Cul-ture Change" coalition now. Together, they are *changing aging*. Part of that means changing the way that people receive care, but it also means helping them understand that there are different types of care out there. Head over to https://www.pioneernetwork.net/ and take a look around to see what I mean.

What it comes down to is that *every person has the right to age gracefully in their own way.* Each person must age on his or her own terms. Our elders shouldn't have to change who they are to fit into a limited array of living options. Instead, their living options should fit them, comfortably and authentically.

So let's look at an overview of what's available, and as we go, I'll continue to share my mother's experience in the hopes that it might illuminate your parent or elder's experience—or help you prepare for what might arise.

LEVEL 1: HOME HEALTH CARE

Homecare is the first, and most minimal, level of care available. Within the homecare umbrella are two divisions: medical and non-medical, which is sometimes called "companion services." If you have a non-medical homecare worker in your home, they cannot do anything medical. This means they cannot dispense medication— they cannot even organize pills for your parent or elder. They can cook; they can clean; they can drive elders to appointments, the grocery store, or the movies. But they are legally prohibited from doing anything medical. Home health non-medical is not usually covered by LTC insurance or Medicare.

A medical homecare worker, on the other hand, can organize and dispense medication. They can administer oxygen or insulin injections. As I began to conduct interviews with families seeking eldercare, I found that concerns about dispensing medication were usually front and center. Remember Steve from Chapter 2? That was the "straw that broke the camel's back" in their family—his parents' medications were being mismanaged. I've seen it in so many families: it's often the number one thing. Home health medical care is usually inverted on some near LTC policies, but not nursing home policies. Medicare can cover this type of care for up to a certain period of time (90 days) or for a specific period of time for rehabilitation.

Taking medication properly is usually the first area where elders find they need help. In my mom's case, she began to get confused. Had she taken her pills when she got up or not? If she knew she had taken pills, she wasn't sure which ones. Sometimes she couldn't remember which pills treated which conditions or why they had been prescribed in the first place. And of course, we had that scare I wrote about earlier where she had to be hospitalized due to overmedication. Just having a homecare worker who checks in daily to manage that single aspect of care can be a huge relief.

It does, however, mean that your parent has to open his or her home to a stranger—or at least a person who starts out as a stranger. For Mom, this was a hurdle we didn't really get beyond. For a short time, I hired a non-medical homecare worker to cook and to take Mom shopping and to get her hair done . . . but Mom never actually went with them.

The worker would arrive, and Mom would say, "Oh, no thanks, I'll wait for my daughter." She just didn't like having this unknown person in her home and in her kitchen!

But I've known other families who loved the arrangement. For the elder, a homecare worker can become a companion and a comfort. The barrier for my mom might simply have been that I live in the same town, so she felt she didn't really need another regular person in her life. She would rather see me. So she would call me and say, "I'm out of dog food!" And I'd go pick some up and bring it to her house—where I'd find that she had bags of it everywhere!

Remaining independent is what matters most to my mom, and that's why we decided ultimately that an independent living situation would be best for her. She feels in control and not as reliant on anyone. Right now that's good for her—it's exactly what she needs at this point in time.

LEVEL 2: INDEPENDENT LIVING

Independent living offers the same level of care as a non-medical homecare worker—but in a community with other elders. Some of these communities are organized like a cul-de-sac; others look like apartment buildings. Sometimes elders just share a house together.

Residents share a space where they meet for meals and recreation, and they have their own or sometimes shared rooms or apartments. Typically, an independent living facility provides one meal per day (usually lunch), and residents can pay for additional meals beyond that.

Residents' rooms or apartments often include a

kitchenette or a full kitchen. Elders who live in independent living are usually at a point in their lives where they can use a stove and cook safely. This leaves them the option of making their own meals if they want to.

Some apartments include a washer and dryer; other independent living facilities might provide laundry services—often at an extra cost. Light housekeeping is usually included.

All independent living facilities will include some kind of safety measure, like pull cords in the kitchen and bathroom, so that if something does happen, elders can pull the cord for help. They can also subscribe to a personal emergency call button, which is worn around the neck.

The emphasis in independent living facilities is on remaining independent and being part of a community. Most will offer recreational activities in addition to shared meals, like exercise, classes, movies, and even on-site hair salons and other services. This is not usually covered by long-term care insurance or Medicare, and is usually private pay, which means the elder pays out of his or her own pocket.

LEVEL 3: ASSISTED LIVING

Assisted living is analogous to the level of care provided by a medical homecare worker—but, again, it is offered at a residential site. As I've mentioned earlier, elders have to qualify for assisted living after being evaluated by a physician. They must be unable to perform two of five basic, daily functions:

- Transferring. This just means being able to get up on their own—either out of a chair or out of bed.
- Using the bathroom.
- Bathing or taking a shower.
- Getting dressed.
- Eating/feeding themselves.

While an elder can decide on her own if and when she wants to move into independent living, she has to have a doctor's recommendation to make the move to assisted living.

In an assisted living facility, healthcare workers will dispense medications to residents and help with other basic medical needs. This is *not* a service that is provided in independent living facilities.

What makes a lot of people nervous about assisted living is the feeling that they might have to surrender to other people's rules and schedules. My mother, for example, likes to sleep late. She usually gets up in time for lunch. If she ever has to be up before 9 o'clock, she loses sleep over it—she's worried she'll sleep through. So, her biggest fear about moving to assisted living has been that they will come in and wake her up at 7 o'clock, make her take her medications, then wheel her down to breakfast at 8 o'clock in the morning when she's not hungry.

This is why it's so essential that organizations like the Pioneer Network are advocating for elders. Again, any kind of living arrangement has to be on the elder's terms. If they don't want to get up at 7 o'clock, fine! If they don't want to eat until noon . . . again, fine!

Assisted living is covered by some LTC policies but not nursing home policies. Veterans and spouses of veterans may be eligible for assistance in paying for this as well. Each community typically has someone on staff to help you find these things out. Be sure to ask.

LEVEL 4: SKILLED NURSING/ADVANCED CARE

As elders begin to need more and more help, skilled nursing comes into play. This means that a skilled nurse is on duty twenty-four hours a day. The nurse is not solely a caregiver but a medical practitioner.

Skilled nursing can also include specialties, such as skilled nursing with a focus on dementia/Alzheimer's care, which requires a very particular knowledge and approach to caregiving. Skilled nursing is covered by long-term care insurance, Medicaid (for those who qualify), and Medicare, though again only for a pre-defined period of time—usually 90 days.

LEVEL 5: HOSPICE

Hospice care is for a person's last stage of life, and can last anywhere from days to weeks to months. It can be set up at home, or there are specific hospice facilities where elders can go and where family members are welcome to visit. This too is covered by LTC, Medicaid, some health insurance policies, and Medicare.

⚜ ⚜ ⚜

The five levels of care are specific enough that it's usually fairly straightforward for families to decide which level their parent needs. The main thing is learning that these different levels exist, so that when you begin the search, you're looking in the right places.

Just learning the difference between the five levels of care can relieve a lot of the anxiety about this new stage of life. So many elders hear "independent living" and picture "assisted living." Or they hear "medical homecare" and think "hospice." If we can get clear about the terms we're using, elders will quickly recognize that these different stages aren't to be feared—and they might even welcome them, just as my mom was delighted to discover that she had a new community of friends when she moved into her independent living facility.

In the next chapter, we'll continue to relieve some of the anxiety of the unknown by talking specifically about how to evaluate your options once you've determined which level of care suits your parent's needs. And we'll continue to look at the real stories of how families have navigated this path and found living situations on their own terms.

CHAPTER 4

Going through the Process:
Know What You're Looking For
and Get Everyone Involved

*H*ARRIET: MY MOTHER was still living in her own house—a tri-level. She had two bad knees and walked around with two canes. Needless to say, her mobility was pretty limited. She was still fairly alert and doing some great things, but we knew Mom's memory was really suffering, and nobody had the courage to have her diagnosed with dementia. And yet, this was clearly an Alzheimer's situation.

We decided to keep her in the house. We thought that's what she wanted: to be in her house, with her things, where she was most comfortable. But that decision was hotly debated by one of my five sisters—the one with medical expertise, incidentally—and my other sisters were split down the middle. The six of us ended up being three on three . . . and it wasn't pretty. There were a lot of heated phone calls and strong words.

The funny thing is, no one had actually asked Mom what *she* wanted. So one day I sat down with her and said, "What do you think about looking into an apartment that would let you have your cats and your freedom?"

And she said, "Let's look at it!"

Astonishingly, we had never really looked at that, because some of my sisters were dead set against it from the start. The irony is that my sisters became the real challenge—my mother was actually ready to take the next step.

We visited some very expensive assisted living apartments, because of course my mother wanted a big place—she didn't want a small room, and of course she had one stipulation she wouldn't budge on: she had to have her cats beside her. Once we took into account the care she'd need, we were looking at spending around $4,000 a month. And then we found this fabulous place in Colorado Springs that took excellent care of their Alzheimer's patients. It was amazing. Mom was really happy there, and the rest of us had a great relationship with the members of the staff.

That was the community where my mom passed away. And we were lucky, because even though she was in that room, we knew she was never alone. She died with her cats on her bed and people around her—and I can smile saying that.

It's really a process, and it was important for my sisters and I to find where we fit in that process. It wasn't always easy for us, because when you're talking about a parent's care, the emotions of the adult children can get dialed up very high. I'm not sure I'll ever be able to mend my relationship with one of my sisters. But at the end of the day, each of us still had a place and a responsibility to get my mother the best care possible. And no matter what your job is—even if it's something that seems small—you still need to be involved.

A few weeks ago, I met with Harriet and two of her sisters. I asked them, "What do you think it would have been like if your mom had sat down with all six of you, way before the onset of her disease, and said, 'This is what I want, this is who's going to be in charge, and this is what you're going to do'? How different do you think things would have been?"

They all said, "Oh my gosh. Like night and day!"

One of Harriet's sisters smiled sadly. "We'd still be a family," she said.

This is why it's so crucial to have a conversation with the elders in your life. It should be the very first thing. Sit down with your mom or dad and ask them: "What do *you* want?" What I want for my mom may be different than what she wants for herself. Maybe I want to put her in an independent living community with a state-of-the-art workout facility, and that's at the top of my priority list. But she doesn't care one whit about the workout facility, because she doesn't work out!

A big part of the process is finding "the right fit." Some elders are simply going to want to stay in their homes. And, barring health issues and safety risks, that might be perfectly okay. My husband's grandmother was a tiny Italian woman who never spoke English and never learned to drive. She lived in a little town in Southern Colorado in a house her husband had built. Every morning, she went across the street to church, and then back home after mass. That's where she wanted to be.

And for many years, she was fine there. She was a very private woman, never much of a socialite, in large part because she couldn't speak the language. So for her, remaining in the home her husband built worked for everyone. When she finally got to the point where she couldn't take care of herself, she moved in with her daughters, but she lived well into her nineties, healthy and strong.

You have to know what you're looking for. And even more importantly, you have to know your elder. What kinds of things do they thrive on? What makes them happy? Let them share with you what *they* want, **before** they get to the point of needing it. Planning ahead helps your mom or dad make more informed choices, and to really become proactive about their own care. Keep the conversation honest, but make it as comfortable as possible—and know what questions to ask. If you don't know what questions to ask, call me and I'll tell you!

In their fantastic resource booklet *Creating Home: A Guide to Better Care Options for an Aging America*, the Pioneer Network has some great suggestions for where to start. Sit down with your siblings and ask the following questions to make sure you're all on the same page. Remember, your brother or sister may have some information you don't, and vice versa.

- Have we talked to our parents about their will, powers of attorney, and end-of-life wishes?

- Are our parents still living on their own?

- Are we worried about their health and/or safety?

- Are we concerned about a cognitive impairment such as Alzheimer's Disease?

- Do we think we should investigate home or long-term care costs/availability?

Once you've answered these questions, you'll have a better sense of where you stand in regards to the kind of care your parents want and need. The next step is to tap into the many resources available to get more information about the types of care available.

Below are just a couple of ideas:

- Contact your Area Agency on Aging or the Eldercare Locator (www.eldercare.org or call 1-800-677-1116) for more information about available services.

- Contact your local ombudsman to learn more about the independent and assisted living communities in your area. An ombudsman is a public advocate, usually appointed by the government, who is charged with representing the interests of the public. If any complaints have been filed against these communities, s/he will know about them.

- Head over to www.CarematchAmerica.com and use our simple search engine. You can find eldercare providers by keyword or location, and you can also search by types of care—from independent living to hospice, and everything in between.

The next step is to start researching the communities themselves. Like Jim said in Chapter 3, you can look at websites till the cows come home, but mostly what you'll see is a picture of the facility's front door. And front doors are nice—but it's far from the whole story. If at all possible, make personal visits to the communities you are considering, *with* your mom and dad. You'll often be able to pick up on the energy of the place from that very first room.

Are elders active and smiling? Are they engaged with their surroundings, rather than staring blankly at a TV? Do they look healthy, physically fit and mentally agile? Does the staff have an easy, positive interaction with the residents?

Your instincts won't tell you everything, so go in armed with a list of specific questions—and don't be afraid to ask every single one. You want to make sure that, not only are your parents getting the best possible care, but they're also getting the best possible care *for their unique situation*.

Here is a list of questions, borrowed from the *Creating Home* book (source: The Pioneer Network), that really get to the heart of the issue. Go through each of these questions with the staff at the communities on your list, and know what to listen for in their replies:

1. **How will you get to know my family member?**
   Listen for: "It is very important for us to really get to know each person who lives here. We have a

questionnaire for your family member to fill out that helps us get started. If they are not able to do this (because of dementia, for example), we want you to help us get to know them. Then we will talk with them and spend time together. We will learn about their preferences, their past, what they enjoy doing now, and their goals and wishes for the future. Everyone on the staff will get to know your family member."

2. **Do the CNAs/nursing assistants take care of the same group of residents each time they work, or do you rotate the assignments after a period of time?**
Listen for: "Consistent Assignment. With few exceptions, our caregivers care for the same group of residents each time they come to work."

3. **What is your policy regarding food choices and alternatives?**
Listen for: "Let me show you a list of the alternatives we always have on hand if someone does not

like the main entrée being offered. Do you think your loved one would be satisfied with these? If not, we can usually accommodate her wishes."

4. **Can my loved one be given a shower/bath when he or she chooses?**

   Listen for: "Yes. We can accommodate a person's lifelong pattern of bathing. Plus, we understand about the special needs of persons with dementia. We have many creative ways to keep people clean, so we can adapt to their preferences and comfort and still maintain cleanliness."

5. **What type of recreational activities are offered here?**

   Listen for: "We offer a wide variety of meaningful and purposeful activities. Residents have input into what is offered. Many of our activities are also spontaneous. Our CNAs do activities with residents based on what the resident likes to do, not only during the day but also at night for those who are awake. We also have someone here in the evenings and on weekends to engage residents."

6. **How do you build a sense of community, and give those who live here a voice in the decisions about how things are done?**

   Listen for: "Residents are part of the home team. We have an active Resident Council. Discussions groups, neighborhood or household meetings are held weekly with residents, staff, and invited family members. Residents have a say in who cares for them."

7. **How do you meet the special needs of people who have some type of dementia?**

   Listen for: "We educate our staff on how to best communicate with people with dementia. Because we have consistent assignments, our staff knows the residents well and can anticipate and meet their needs in flexible, creative ways. We also support and teach staff how to problem-solve difficult situations."

8. **What is the role of family members? Do you have a Family Council?**

   Listen for: "Family members may visit here any time, volunteer, and participate in our Family

Council. Let me provide you with information on a Family Council meeting, so you can sit in and see the ways our elders' families are actively involved in their care.

This is far from a comprehensive list, but it will go a long way toward helping you ask the right questions, and listening closely to the replies. If you sense any reticence or annoyance as you are moving through your list, or get any inkling that the staff is unwilling or unable to accommodate special needs, preferences, or requests, chances are the community is not the right one for your parent.

Remember Jim from Chapter 3, who was searching for an independent living community for his home? In our interviews, he said something I will never forget, something so powerful and profound it became the title of this book. "It's as simple as where you live," Jim said.

It's true for you—and it's true for the elders you love.

CHAPTER 5

How Carematch America Can Help

*I*N MY JOB, I present to and teach the owners and marketing people from the facilities and communities dedicated to eldercare. My goal is to teach them how to be better listeners, to truly listen and understand the keywords consumers say. This is the foundation of "consumer-based care." These facilities function as homes and communities, yes, but they are also businesses, part of a much larger eldercare industry. Like any business, the most fulfilling transaction happens when the consumer is informed—and when the provider knows what the consumer wants before they even show up, so they can have a little bit more of their hearts.

My interviews with Steve, Jim, and Harriet were a part of this process. I show the video of these interviews at every presentation I give so that the marketing teams get an insight into what it is people *really* want for their parents. What are the keywords that come up when they talk? What are they looking for?

I have the marketers write down the keywords they hear as Steve, Jim, and Harriet are speaking. Then we compare the list to the keywords that appear on most of the flyers and advertising for these communities. It may surprise you that the lists rarely match up.

The elders' children talk about things like *community, safety, purpose, activity,* and *engagement.* The brochures focus on things like *workout room* and *flat-screen TV.* I can't tell you how many brochures I've seen where the flat-screen television is front and center. So often, that's what the marketing people think is important: all the glitz and glamour their nice new facility can offer. Who cares?

What family members are looking at isn't the TV in the main room—it's the man sitting in front of it. Does he look like a happy guy? No, he most certainly does not. He looks sour and sedentary. But flip to the inside of the brochure, where they've buried a picture of a smiling white-haired woman in a wheelchair playing volleyball with a little boy. Now *that's* what people care about. That woman should be on the front page!

It is my great joy to teach marketers about consumer-based care. They don't need to market their televisions; they need to respond to the keywords people like Harriet, Steve, and Jim are using. These are the things people truly care about.

As I try to impress on the marketing teams at my workshops, you're not just marketing to the elder whom you are trying to entice to join your community. You've got to understand the dynamics of the *whole family*. It's crucial to keep that connectedness a part of the elder's life. It isn't just about the best care you can give; it's about how to keep that elder connected to his or her family, and how to pave the way for the entire family to come visit and be a part of their loved one's life.

In every presentation, I move through the three stages of eldercare:

- The need for care
- The search for care

And ultimately:

- Success!

The work I'm doing matters to me. This isn't some obscure theoretical pursuit, and I'm not just some corporate person who is trying to become a millionaire on a website. I've lived this story. I'm living it with my mom right now. That's what Carematch America is all about: a real story, a real person, and a real passion to help others through what can otherwise be a difficult and uncertain process.

The people who come to our website realize they are not alone. They find other people who understand what they are going through, and they discover ways to build their own showcases, building the foundation for a true "care match": when what the consumer wants is in alignment with what the provider can offer.

If you've enjoyed what you've read here, I invite you to continue the conversation. Visit www.Carematch America.com for more information, or contact me directly at Carol@CarematchAmerica.com. I'd be honored to help you on your journey.

If you're new to the process, take heart: it *is* possible to find the right care options for your parents, to help them age with grace, warmth, and dignity. Taking care of the elders who have taken care of you is one of the greatest gifts life can offer. I wish you nothing but joy along the journey.

CPSIA information can be obtained
at www.ICGtesting.com
Printed in the USA
FSOW02n1508250816
23994FS